IMAGES
of America

FORT BRIDGER

On the Cover: Capt. Anson Mills, post commander at Fort Bridger in 1866, forced soldiers to publicly sit astride a wooden horse in an effort to embarrass them and curb minor infractions. "This method of punishment proved most efficient," Mills later recalled, "as the men soon came to dread 'riding the horse' a good deal more then they did spending a month in the guardhouse." (Courtesy National Archives.)

IMAGES
of America

FORT BRIDGER

Ephriam D. Dickson III and Mark J. Nelson

ARCADIA
PUBLISHING

ISBN 978-1-4671-3145-2

Published by Arcadia Publishing
Charleston, South Carolina

Printed in the United States of America

Library of Congress Control Number: 2014932942

For all general information, please contact Arcadia Publishing:
Telephone 843-853-2070
Fax 843-853-0044
E-mail sales@arcadiapublishing.com
For customer service and orders:
Toll-Free 1-888-313-2665

Visit us on the Internet at www.arcadiapublishing.com

Dedicated to the memory of John H. Hamilton.

Contents

Acknowledgments

This book would not have been possible without the assistance and support of many individuals who help preserve the history of Fort Bridger and the surrounding region. We would especially like to thank the staff at Fort Bridger State Historic Site, including superintendent Linda Newman-Byers and curator Cecil Sanderson. Former Fort Bridger site manager Tom Lindmier has also shared his wealth of knowledge about the fort. Cindy Brown and Suzi Taylor of the Wyoming State Archives helped locate images in the state archives, and Ruth Lauritzen, Brigida Blasi, and Cyndi McCullers from the Sweetwater County Historical Museum allowed the use of photographs in their institution's collection. We also thank Butch and Nancy Kahus of Fort Bridger for sharing their photographs and information about the post.

INTRODUCTION

During the 19th century, commercial photographers traveled throughout the West in an effort to secure images for sale to an interested public back East. Despite its remote location in southwestern Wyoming, Fort Bridger witnessed a number of these itinerate artists stopping briefly to set up their cameras and record portraits and landscape views.

John W. Jones passed through Fort Bridger in the fall of 1851 while producing a series of daguerreotypes along the trail from California; however, none of his images are known to have survived. During the Utah War of 1857–1858, David A. Burr fled from Salt Lake City with his father, the surveyor general for Utah Territory, and spent a portion of that winter at Fort Bridger and nearby Camp Scott. The 20-year-old photographer's small number of surviving images show Army life in this cantonment of log cabins and tents. In 1858, photographer Samuel C. Mills accompanied the Army's reinforcements to Utah as a member of Capt. James H. Simpson's exploratory expedition. Passing through Fort Bridger in September 1858, he produced the earliest surviving view of the stone Mormon fort.

During the 1860s, Fort Bridger was visited by several Salt Lake City photographers, including Charles R. Savage and Charles W. Carter, who were creating portfolios of Western views. Union Pacific photographer Andrew J. Russell also passed through Fort Bridger while documenting the railroad's construction activities, and William Henry Jackson stopped here briefly in 1870 as part of a government survey. A small number of photographs have also survived from the camera of Pvt. Charles Howard, a soldier who operated a photographic gallery at Fort Bridger from about 1875 to 1877.

Improvements in the technology soon put cameras in the hands of hobbyists. In the last years of Fort Bridger, several residents are known to have had small cameras, including a daughter of Judge Carter as well as Lt. Charles P. Stivers. By the early 20th century, further developments in cameras and film along with the completion of the Lincoln Highway and the birth of tourism made it possible for visitors to Fort Bridger to produce their own souvenir images of the historic post.

Through the work of these early photographers, readers can now see Fort Bridger as they did, changing from a remote trading post to an emigrant way station, then from a frontier military post to a small ranching community.

Jim Bridger. Born in Virginia, Bridger came West in 1822 at age 18 and spent the next two decades engaged in the fur trade. In 1843, he established a trading post on the Blacks Fork of the Green River that soon bore his name. (Courtesy Wyoming State Archives.)

One

Before the Army

Rock art and stone artifacts testify to the fact that people have lived in southwestern Wyoming for thousands of years. By the early 18th century, a new wave of native people had pushed into the region from the west, forefathers of a tribe that eventually became known as the Shoshone. Over the next two centuries, this tribe expanded its influence eastward to the rich buffalo grounds of the northern plains. But by the late 18th century, successive waves of other native emigrants arriving from the east—including the Arapaho, the Cheyenne, and finally the Lakota—pushed the Shoshone back into their mountain strongholds in present Wyoming.

White fur traders arrived in the early 19th century. Seeking the pelts of the elusive beaver, these men plied the cold mountain streams throughout the Rocky Mountains. They gathered for the annual rendezvous, including several held in the Green River Valley, where they traded for supplies and enjoyed a raucous social gathering. Changes in styles back East, the importation of cheaper furs from South America, and the overhunting of beaver in the Rocky Mountains brought an end to the fur trade, leaving mountain men searching for new opportunities.

After two decades as a fur trader, Jim Bridger decided to establish a trading post on the Blacks Fork along the newly developed emigrant road to the Pacific coast. By 1843, Fort Bridger offered a variety of supplies to passing wagon trains, as well as blacksmithing and replacement livestock. Edwin Bryant stopped here in July 1846, describing it as "two or three miserable log-cabins, rudely constructed, and bearing but a faint resemblance to habitable houses." Several mountain men also operated toll ferries for emigrants crossing the Green River.

The migration of Mormon converts to the Salt Lake Valley starting in 1847 altered events in the Fort Bridger area. In 1850, Fort Bridger was included within the boundaries of the newly created Utah Territory. Conflict between the mountain men and Mormon leadership over control of the ferries resulted in Brigham Young deciding to establish a community in the vicinity of the Green River and eventually assuming control of Fort Bridger itself.

EASTERN SHOSHONE VILLAGE NEAR SOUTH PASS. With some access to Great Plains buffalo herds, the Eastern Shoshone depended upon their horses to move hide lodges and other household items as they migrated through the region. This photograph was taken by William Henry Jackson in 1870. (Courtesy Smithsonian Institution.)

SHOSHONE WOMEN. By the early 1870s, various trade blankets were quickly supplanting buffalo robes for personal wear, while canvas had largely replaced hide lodges. These manufactured items were made available to the Shoshone through trade and at an annual issue by the Office of Indian Affairs, both conducted at Fort Bridger. (Courtesy National Archives.)

Chief Washakie. Under the able leadership of Chief Washakie, the Eastern Shoshone generally maintained good relations with the communities in the Fort Bridger area. This portrait was taken by William H. Jackson near South Pass around 1870. (Courtesy Wyoming State Archives.)

Encampment near South Pass. "Every spring the Shoshones of the North and the Utes from the South used to gather on the neutral ground at Fort Bridger," recalled Dr. James Corson, "and trade the buffalo robes of the former for the blankets and other products of the latter." (Courtesy Wyoming State Archives.)

Indian Camp. While at Fort Bridger in 1870, photographer William H. Jackson took his camera to the nearby Shoshone village to secure several glass negatives of the people and their lodges. (Courtesy Library of Congress.)

Rocky Mountain Trapper. During the early 19th century, a number of individuals of various nationalities arrived in the Green River region trapping beaver for resale. By the late 1830s, however, this animal had been nearly hunted out of the Wind River Mountains. This is a lithograph based on an 1844 painting by Charles Deas. (Courtesy Library of Congress.)

Green River Rendezvous. The annual rendezvous allowed trappers to sell their pelts and to resupply. Though he was too young to have attended a rendezvous, photographer William H. Jackson later painted his idea of what this event must have been like, with the Wind River Mountains in the background. (Courtesy Wyoming State Archives.)

Jim Bridger. "I have established a small fort, with a blacksmith shop and a supply of iron on the road of the emigrants on Black's Fork of Green River," Bridger wrote in 1843, adding that he expected "considerable business in that way with them, and [to] establish trade with the Indians in the neighborhood." (Courtesy Wyoming State Archives.)

Pierre Louis Vasquez. As a business partner with Bridger, Louis Vasquez helped establish Fort Bridger. He later operated a store in Salt Lake City and then retired to Westport, Missouri, where he died in 1868. (Courtesy Utah State Historical Society.)

Fort Bridger, Black's Fork of Green River. Capt. Howard Stansbury arrived at Fort Bridger in 1849. "It is built in the usual form, of pickets, with the lodging apartments and office opening into a hollow square," Stansbury noted. This sketch of Bridger's trading post was included in Stansbury's official report. (Courtesy National Archives.)

Uncle Jack. Coming west with the fur trade as a young man, John Robertson—or Uncle Jack Robinson as he was also known—settled in the Fort Bridger area with his Indian family. He served as the Shoshone interpreter during the 1863 treaty negotiations. Uncle Jack died in 1884 and was buried in the Fort Bridger cemetery. (Courtesy National Archives.)

Wagon Train on the Big Sandy River. In 1844, a new section of the Oregon-California Trail known as the Greenwood Cutoff was pioneered across the Big Sandy, threatening to divert emigrant traffic away from Fort Bridger. "From the Big Sandy to Green River, a distance of thirty-five miles, there is not a drop of water," warned one published trail guide. (Courtesy LDS Church History Library.)

James and Margret Reed. Arriving at Fort Bridger in July 1846, James Reed purchased two oxen from Vasquez and Bridger, referring to them as "the only fair traders in these parts." Leaving the main trail here, the Donner-Reed party followed the new Hastings Cutoff across the difficult Salt Lake desert, losing valuable time that tragically trapped them in the Sierra Nevada Mountains in winter. (Courtesy Utah State Historical Society.)

BRIGHAM YOUNG. In 1847, Brigham Young led the first party of Latter-Day Saints (or Mormons) past Fort Bridger en route to the Salt Lake Valley where they established their new Zion. Over the next several years, thousands of Mormon converts passed through Fort Bridger on their way to Salt Lake City. This portrait is by Marsena Cannon, done in 1850. (Courtesy LDS Church History Library.)

ORSON PRATT. Part of the Mormons' 1847 "vanguard party," Mormon leader Orson Pratt described Bridger's fort as "two adjoining log houses, dirt roofs, and a small picket yard of logs set in the ground, about 8 feet high." Pratt also noted, "Mosquitoes very numerous and troublesome." (Courtesy LDS Church History Library.)

Wagons in Echo Canyon. The establishment of Salt Lake City drew many new emigrants past Bridger's trading post on their way to the valley. Among the dramatic sections of this road was Echo Canyon with its towering red cliffs. (Courtesy LDS Church History Library.)

Bluffs in Echo Canyon. Photographer Samuel C. Mills captured the earliest known image from Echo Canyon during his trip through in 1858. Known later as the Devil's Post Office, this particular rock outcropping was later the site of a Pony Express station. (Courtesy Library of Congress.)

Bill Hickman. In 1853, Brigham Young sent Hickman to the Green River near Fort Bridger to establish a church-owned ferry, but after encountering intense and sometimes violent competition between mountain men and other Mormons for ferry business, he decided to operate a trading post near South Pass instead. (Courtesy LDS Church History Library.)

James Ferguson. To gain control of the Fort Bridger area, Brigham Young requested an arrest warrant for Jim Bridger on the charges of illegal trading with Indians. In August 1853, sheriff and militia officer James Ferguson was dispatched with a company of men to arrest Bridger and to seize any weapons or liquor found at the trading post. (Courtesy Will Bagley.)

Orson Hyde. A member of the LDS Church's Quorum of Twelve, Hyde was selected by Brigham Young to organize the Green River Mission in 1853. He then named nearly 100 men who moved to Fort Bridger in two companies. (Courtesy LDS Church History Library.)

FORT SUPPLY. Encountering resistance from angry mountain men, the first Mormon companies established a new fortified settlement about 12 miles away named Fort Supply. "When our blockhouse was completed," noted one of the party, "we felt safer than ever." (Courtesy Wyoming State Archives.)

HOSEA STOUT. Among those called to the Green River Mission was 43-year-old lawyer Hosea Stout. "This is the most forbidding and godforsaken place I have ever seen for an attempt to be made for a settlement," he recorded in his diary after arriving at Fort Bridger in May 1853. (Courtesy Utah State Historical Society.)

Isaac Bullock. Crossing the plains in 1852, Bullock was selected as one of the leaders for the Green River Mission the following year. Over the next two years, he studied the Shoshone language and negotiated with Chief Washakie over Mormon presence in the region. (Courtesy Utah State Historical Society.)

Lewis Robison. While the claim remains controversial, Robison apparently purchased Fort Bridger from the old fur trapper and his partner Vasquez in August 1855. Robinson continued to operate the trading station for the next two years. (Courtesy LDS Church Archives.)

Remnants of the Mormon Fortifications. In the spring of 1857, Lewis Robison built a tall cobblestone fortification at Fort Bridger, 100 feet square with an adjoining horse corral. One Mormon attending a celebration of its completion noted its "strong walls 16 feet high and five feet thick." (Courtesy Utah State Historical Society.)

Wagons on the Road. During this period, emigrants continued to travel the roads through the Fort Bridger area. Many California-bound travelers chose to winter in the Salt Lake Valley before continuing their journey while Mormon pioneers continued to pass en route to their new home. Supplies and livestock could be purchased at Fort Bridger for the next leg of the journey. (Courtesy LDS Church History Library.)

Sibley Tent at Camp Scott. To protect the troops camped near Fort Bridger during the winter of 1857–1858, the Army issued a new experimental tent known as the Sibley. This conical canvas structure was modeled after a Comanche lodge and allowed soldiers to enjoy a simple sheet iron stove inside. (Courtesy Utah State Archives).

Two

The Utah War

Concerned that Mormon leaders in Utah Territory were bordering on rebellion, newly elected president James Buchanan decided to replace Brigham Young as territorial governor and ordered a large column of troops to the region to reestablish federal authority. In August 1857, over 1,500 soldiers departed Fort Leavenworth, Kansas, beginning their three-month trek to Utah.

Learning of the approaching Army, Brigham Young ordered Fort Bridger burned and the Mormon communities withdrawn. As the federal troops neared the Green River, the Mormon militia captured and burned three of its wagon trains. The arrival of winter and the loss of livestock and supplies forced the Army into a winter cantonment at Fort Bridger, huddled inside their tents on half rations waiting until spring for reinforcements and additional supplies. In the meantime, diplomacy prevailed. Peace commissioners successfully negotiated a settlement that avoided an open conflict between Mormon forces and the Army.

While most of the troops departed for Salt Lake City in June 1858, two companies of the 6th Infantry and one of the 1st Cavalry were ordered to remain behind at Fort Bridger to establish a permanent military post. Soldiers began cutting logs in the Uinta Mountains and constructing quarters and warehouses. "The soldiers stationed at Fort Bridger have a perfect little paradise of their own in the midst of a howling wilderness," noted one correspondent several months later. "Several streams of clear, cold water roll through the valley in which it is built, and everything necessary to a soldier's comfort, with what the government gives him, is to be found. The Mormons in the neighborhood bring daily into the Fort, and sell, at pretty fair prices, all kinds of vegetables and fruit to be found at this season of the year."

As the Civil War began, federal troops were withdrawn from most military posts throughout the West. Fort Crittenden, located southwest of Salt Lake City, was abandoned. Most of the troops at Fort Bridger except a small handful of enlisted men were sent back East to fight the Confederacy. For many observers, this appeared to be the end of the military's role at Fort Bridger.

Pres. James Buchanan. A southern Democrat with extensive political experience, Buchanan was inaugurated as the 15th president of the United States in March 1857. One of his first major policy decisions was to replace Brigham Young as the governor of the Utah Territory. (Courtesy Library of Congress.)

John B. Floyd. Selected by President Buchanan to serve as the secretary of war, Floyd was charged with sending a large military force to Utah to ensure the peaceful transfer of the governorship and to reestablish federal authority in the territory. (Courtesy Library of Congress.)

Gen. Winfield Scott. As general-in-chief of the US Army, Scott determined which troops could be spared from their earlier assignments, and in May 1857, he ordered about 2,500 men to march to Utah Territory. (Courtesy Library of Congress.)

Gen. Thomas S. Jesup. Organizing the extensive logistics required for the Utah Expedition was the responsibility of the Army's quartermaster general. Jesup and his staff assembled the quantity of military supplies needed for an entire year and contracted for its transportation to Utah. (Courtesy National Archives.)

Gen. William S. Harney. Command of the Utah Expedition was initially given to General Harney, known as a stern disciplinarian. He had previously led a punitive expedition against the Lakota or Sioux that earned him a reputation as a hard campaigner. The governor of the Kansas Territory, however, protested the general's departure from his territory during this period of great civil unrest over slavery. (Courtesy Library of Congress.)

GEN. ALBERT S. JOHNSTON. In August 1857, as the troops departed Fort Leavenworth, command of the Utah Expedition was transferred to Johnston. Arriving from Texas via Washington, DC, he raced overland with a small escort to catch up with the lead elements of his advancing columns. (Courtesy National Archives.)

Gathering in Big Cottonwood Canyon. During the Mormons' 10th annual Pioneer Day celebration held in Big Cottonwood Canyon on July 24, 1857, Brigham Young formally announced that the Army was approaching. "If the United States sends out troops to fight us this season," he said the following week, "we shall whip them out." (Courtesy John Eldredge.)

Daniel H. Wells. As commander of the territorial militia or Nauvoo Legion, Wells ordered men forward to harass the approaching Army by burning the grass and running off livestock. They also built defensive fortifications in Echo Canyon. As Mormon settlers evacuated the Green River area, Fort Bridger was burned on the evening of October 2. (Courtesy John Eldredge.)

Burning of Army Supplies. In early October 1857, three separate wagon trains with a total of 76 wagons transporting Army supplies were captured and burned by a detachment of the Nauvoo Legion led by Maj. Lot Smith. (Courtesy John Eldredge.)

Tents Near Camp Scott. Following heavy snow that slowed the Army's advancement to a crawl, Colonel Johnston ordered his troops back to Fort Bridger, where they erected tents along the banks of the Black's Fork at what became known as Camp Scott. Here, the Army spent a long winter on half rations waiting for the arrival of replacement animals and reinforcements. (Courtesy LDS Church History Library.)

FORT BRIDGER, 1858. Within the burned-out walls of the Mormon fortification at Fort Bridger, the Army erected tents and temporary structures to store all of its supplies. Elevated artillery

platforms known as lunettes were erected at two corners of the fort. This photograph was taken by Samuel C. Mills. (Courtesy Library of Congress.)

Pulling the Firewood Wagon. Having lost most of their mules and horses from exposure to the bitter cold and a lack of proper foraging, soldiers were left to pull their own wagons by hand while collecting firewood, as shown in this photograph attributed to David A. Burr taken near Fort Bridger. (Courtesy Utah State Historical Society.)

Capt. Randolph B. Marcy. In an effort to secure replacement horses and mules, Captain Marcy was sent on a dangerous and arduous winter journey south from Fort Bridger to Fort Massachusetts, a small log stockade located in what is today southern Colorado. Marcy successfully returned in the spring with fresh horses and reinforcements. (Courtesy Library of Congress.)

Fort Leavenworth, 1858. To reinforce Johnston's troops, General Scott ordered additional troops to Utah Territory. In the spring of 1858, a total of 3,000 officers and enlisted men gathered at Fort Leavenworth in preparation of marching to Utah. In this view by Samuel C. Mills, the original Fort Leavenworth blockhouse can be seen in the background. (Courtesy Library of Congress.)

Gen. Persifor F. Smith. Command of the new column of troops was assigned to 60-year-old Gen. P.F. Smith; however, he died at Fort Leavenworth in May and command of the expedition passed to General Harney. (Courtesy National Archives.)

Ecklesville. This early image, presumably taken by David Burr, shows some of the tents occupied by the civilian territorial officials camped near the Army during the winter of 1857–1858. A mixture of Army tents, Indian lodges, and primitive cottonwood log cabins are visible, a testament to the primitive nature of accommodations that winter near Fort Bridger. (Courtesy LDS Church History Library.)

Thomas Kane. Traveling to Utah without official sanction from the federal government, Kane nonetheless attempted to broker a peace settlement between Brigham Young in Salt Lake City and federal officials at Fort Bridger to avoid bloodshed. This portrait was produced later during the Civil War when Kane served as a brigadier general in the Army of the Potomac. (Courtesy John Eldredge.)

Gov. Alfred Cumming. A native of Georgia, Cumming accompanied the Army to Utah to serve as the next territorial governor, spending the winter with his wife in tents near Fort Bridger. In March 1858, at the urging of Thomas Kane, the new governor traveled into Salt Lake City ahead of the Army, causing a widening rift with military authorities. (Courtesy Utah State Historical Society.)

Camp Near Fort Bridger. These primitive log buildings were probably also part of the encampments near Fort Bridger occupied during the Utah War. (Courtesy LDS Church History Library.)

Regimental Band. At least two of the regiments that marched to Utah Territory brought their regimental band, providing music and entertainment at this remote station. The photograph is attributed to David A. Burr, between 1857–1858. (Courtesy Utah State Historical Society.)

Marching Through Salt Lake City. After securing additional horses and mules, General Johnston departed Fort Bridger just as peace negotiations with Mormon leaders were completed. On June 26, 1858, the troops peacefully marched through the deserted streets of Salt Lake City past the Beehive and Lion House, marking the end of the Utah War. (Courtesy John Eldredge.)

Fort Kearny, 1858. By the end of the Utah War, three military forts now protected the section of the emigrant trail from Nebraska to Utah. Located along the Platte River, Fort Kearny was described by one Utah War officer as "as miserable a hole," with quarters built of sod "too open for human beings to live in." (Courtesy Library of Congress.)

Fort Laramie, 1858. Established initially as a fur trading post, Fort Laramie was purchased by the Army in 1849 and had provided support and protection for emigrants on the trail. During the Utah War, supplies from this fort were hurried forward in the spring of 1858 for Johnston's troops at Fort Bridger. (Courtesy Library of Congress.)

Maj. Gen. Edward R.S. Canby. As a major in the 10th Infantry, Canby came west with the Utah Expedition in 1857. He served as post commander at Fort Bridger for nearly two years beginning in August 1858 and oversaw the garrison's initial construction. Canby was killed in northeastern California in 1873 while negotiating peace with the Modoc Indians. This portrait is by Mathew Brady in 1864. (Courtesy Library of Congress.)

OFFICERS' QUARTERS. Following the departure of General Johnston's troops in June 1858, three companies were left at Fort Bridger to establish a permanent military post. For the next two years, logs were hauled down from the Uinta Mountains to construct buildings such as this row of duplex officers' quarters. (Courtesy LDS Church History Library.)

MORMON FORT REUSED. While log barracks and officers' quarters were constructed at Fort Bridger, the old Mormon fortification continued to serve as the storehouse for quartermaster and commissary stores as well as a corral for government animals. This drawing was created in September 1858 by Pvt. Henry Sommer, 7th Infantry. (Courtesy Fielding L. Tyler.)

Dr. Roberts Bartholow. In 1858, a year after becoming an Army surgeon, Dr. Bartholow was transferred to Fort Bridger where he supervised the construction of the first post hospital. He resigned from the Army during the Civil War to become a professor at the Ohio Medical College in Cincinnati. In addition to authoring a number of medical texts, Dr. Bartholow is best known for his controversial experiment stimulating a patient's brain with electricity. (Courtesy National Library of Medicine.)

The Sutler Store. Located on the edge of the new garrison, the sutler store offered a wide range of products and services to the officers and enlisted men at Fort Bridger. William A. Carter was appointed post sutler at Fort Bridger in 1858 and remained in this role until his death in 1881. (Courtesy Wyoming State Archives.)

Sir Richard F. Burton. In 1860, this famous British explorer stopped briefly at Fort Bridger on his way to Salt Lake City. "The officers complained very naturally of their isolation and unpleasant duty," Burton wrote, "which principally consists in keeping the roads open for, and the Indians from cutting off, parties of unmanageable emigrants, who look upon the federal Army as their humblest servants." (Courtesy National Archives.)

Joseph C. Clark Jr., First Lieutenant. As the Army withdrew from Utah Territory at the beginning of the Civil War in 1861, 1st Lt. Clark was placed in command at Fort Bridger with just nine soldiers to protect the remaining supplies. After multiple requests to be relieved, he was finally allowed to depart to rejoin his artillery company for the war. (Courtesy Vern DeLong.)

Officers at Fort Bridger. Standing outside their log quarters along Officers' Row, these men pose for the camera of railroad photographer Andrew J. Russell in 1868. The ever present sutler, William A. Carter, stands in the center with his hallmark beard. (Courtesy Wyoming State Archives.)

Three

Return of the Army

As the Civil War raged back East, volunteer troops from California under the command of Col. Patrick Edward Connor were sent to protect the main overland road across Nevada and Utah Territory. In 1862, Connor established Camp Ruby in central Nevada, Camp Douglas on the outskirts of Salt Lake City, and in December of that year he sent troops to reoccupy Fort Bridger. Following Connor's devastating attack on a Shoshone camp on the Bear River in January 1863, the eastern bands, including that of Chief Washakie, met at Fort Bridger to negotiate a peace treaty. Volunteer troops stationed at Fort Bridger continued to patrol the trail even after the Civil War ended until they were finally relieved by federal troops in 1866.

The discovery of gold in the Wind River Range sparked a rush in 1867 in the area that became known as the Sweetwater Mining District. To protect gold miners from the threat of attack by Native Americans, soldiers from Fort Bridger were dispatched to the area on periodic detached service. On May 4, 1870, the men of Company D, 2nd Cavalry engaged a superior force of Arapaho warriors near Atlantic City resulting in the death of 1st Lt. C.B. Stambaugh and the wounding of Sgt. Alexander Brown.

From 1866 to 1868, detachments from Fort Bridger also provided protection for survey and construction parties along the new Union Pacific Railroad, passing just nine miles north of the post. When Wyoming Territory was created in 1868, Fort Bridger and the upper Green River Valley were included within its boundaries. The next decade was one of calm military routine.

"There was a sort of homie feeling about Fort Bridger such as I had never before found at a Post," recalled Dr. Joseph K. Corson who served as a surgeon there in the 1870s. "It was a small garrison, three companies and a very healthy one and a pleasant contrast after the large post I had been serving at." While the railroad improved the ability to ship supplies to Fort Bridger, this new transportation network ultimately contributed to the demise of the famed frontier post.

Robert T. Burton. In the spring of 1862, Shoshone raids east of Fort Bridger prompted the acting governor of Utah Territory to order a company of the Nauvoo Legion under Colonel Burton to patrol the trail. "The company is composed of picked men, the cream of the regiment that could be spared," noted a Salt Lake City correspondent. "Brigham has sent two of his own sons and a son-in-law, and Heber [Kimball] has two of his sons in it." (Courtesy Utah State Historical Society.)

Lot Smith. Two days after Colonel Burton's departure, a telegram arrived from the War Department addressed directly to Brigham Young, requesting a company of cavalry for 90 days' federal service patrolling the trail. Departing on May 1 under the command of Capt. Lot Smith, the company passed back and forth between Fort Bridger and Independence Rock. (Courtesy John Eldredge.)

Gen. P. Edward Connor. In December 1862, two months after establishing a military post near Salt Lake City, Connor sent one company of the 3rd California Volunteer Infantry to reoccupy Fort Bridger as part of the government's effort to provide military protection along the main emigrant trail west to California. (Courtesy National Archives.)

Capt. Willard Kittredge. Initially a first lieutenant, Kittredge reestablished the military presence at Fort Bridger in 1862 and served as the post commander on several occasions over the next two years. His daughter Charmain later married the famous author Jack London. (Courtesy University of Utah.)

SAGWITCH AND WIFE. A prominent leader among the Northwestern Shoshone, Sagwitch was encamped on the Bear River near present Prescott, Idaho, in January 1863 when Connor's troops attacked the village, killing more than 200 individuals. Sagwitch survived and later became a Mormon elder. (Courtesy LDS Church History Library.)

WASHAKIE. In the wake of the Bear River Massacre, most of the Shoshone leaders signed treaties with the United States, bringing an end to the conflict. As one of the key spokesmen for the Eastern Shoshone, Washakie signed the treaty at Fort Bridger in July 1863. (Courtesy Wyoming State Archives.)

LUTHER H. MANN JR. Appointed Indian agent for the Eastern Shoshone in 1861, Mann was present at Fort Bridger for the 1863 treaty and oversaw the distribution of food and clothing. In 1868–1869, he supervised the transfer of the tribe to the newly established Wind River Reservation in central Wyoming. (Courtesy Bancroft Library.)

Fort Bridger. Some sense of the remoteness of Fort Bridger is afforded by this general view of the post taken by photographer Charles W. Carter during the winter of 1866–1867. In the coming years, trees were planted to help soften the barrenness of the landscape. (Courtesy Wyoming State Archives.)

View Across the Parade Ground. The flagstaff stood at the upper end of the parade grounds near the row of officers' quarters. "At 12 [noon] the flag was run up on a beautiful staff, which had just been erected," noted Capt. Richard Gatlin in February 1860. "This flag flies higher above the sea than any in the United States, this place being about the elevation of South Pass—7000 feet." (Courtesy Wyoming State Archives.)

Officers' Quarters. Built in 1858, each of these buildings provided housing for two officers and their families, with kitchen attachments added in 1870 on the rear. Officers' Row continued in use through the entire history of the fort. (Courtesy Wyoming State Archives.)

Quartermaster Office. During the 1860s, this log building served as headquarters for the quartermaster department at the post, responsible for the maintenance of all buildings, managing the Army's horse and mule herd as well as overseeing the storage and issue of uniforms and other military supplies. (Courtesy Wyoming State Archives.)

Ruins of the Old Mormon Fort. A significant portion of the original Mormon fortification was still in use by the Army as warehouses to store quartermaster and commissary supplies and equipment into the late 1860s. The post's first commissary building is also visible on the right. (Courtesy Wyoming State Archives.)

Ration Day at Fort Bridger. Enlisted soldiers were provided with a basic ration of meat, bread, and beans issued about every two weeks from the commissary building. The food was prepared by each company in their own kitchen. (Courtesy Wyoming State Archives.)

Soldiers in Formation. Each morning, the enlisted soldiers of Fort Bridger fell into formation in dress uniform for roll call and a changing of the guard ceremony. The men again fell into formation each evening for retreat as the flag was brought down for the day, part of the daily ritual of every military post. (Courtesy Wyoming State Archives.)

Bridger Butte. Just west of Fort Bridger, photographer Charles W. Carter captured this winter view of Bridger Butte, one of the landmarks for travelers on the road to Salt Lake City. (Courtesy Wyoming State Archives.)

WILLIAM A. CARTER. Initially a partner of Livingston & Kinkead, Carter came west with the Utah Expedition in 1857 and was appointed as the official sutler at Fort Bridger the following year. In addition to his store at Fort Bridger, Carter was also involved in a wide range of other economic activities in the region including ranching, freighting, and lumber. He also served as the probate judge for the county. (Courtesy Wyoming State Archives.)

SUTLER'S STORE. As the only authorized mercantile establishment at Fort Bridger, Carter's store carried a wide range of goods, such as canned foods, medicine, alcohol, and bolts of cloth. Customers included not only the soldiers, officers, and their families from the post but also cattlemen and travelers through the area. (Courtesy Wyoming State Archives.)

Sutler's Residence. In the summer of 1859, Judge Carter brought his family to Fort Bridger and they lived in their home adjacent to the store. Visitors often commented on his congenial manner as well as his fine food and large library. (Courtesy Wyoming State Archives.)

"The Lodge." Among Judge Carter's most important employees at his store was his son-in-law James Van Allen Carter (far right). His brother-in-law, Richard Hamilton (far left), worked with Carter primarily in his cattle and logging endeavors. The men appear to be enjoying coffee as part of their informal mess group. (Courtesy Wyoming State Archives.)

"ALL ABOARD!" Financier Ben Holliday operated the Overland Stage Line from 1862 to 1866, with stage stations located every 10 to 12 miles along the route to provide fresh horses and sometimes food for weary passengers. Here the stage stops briefly outside the station at Fort Bridger. (Courtesy Wyoming State Archives.)

LT. COL. ORVILLE E. BABCOCK. As a member of General Grant's staff and an inspector for the Army, Babcock examined Fort Bridger in June 1866 and expressed his concern about its "shameful condition—grounds not policed, buildings out of order, flooring burned up, bridges burned, shade trees broken down." (Courtesy Library of Congress.)

Capt. Andrew S. Burt. Arriving at Fort Bridger in July 1866, Captain Burt assumed command of the post. "Three months of tent life had not made us critical of our new surroundings," his wife later recalled, "although the post was not in particularly good repair." The arrival of Burt's company marked the return of the regular Army to Fort Bridger. (Courtesy National Archives.)

Capt. Anson Mills. Captain Mills took over as post commander at Fort Bridger in November 1866. During his time on post, he devised a looped belt for soldiers to hold metallic ammunition cartridges, the patent for which, along with his later designs, earned him a small fortune. (Courtesy National Archives.)

South Pass City. In 1867, the discovery of gold about 150 miles northeast of Fort Bridger attracted a large influx of miners and merchants who established several boomtowns such as South Pass City. Detachments from Fort Bridger were initially called to patrol the area following several raids by the Shoshone. In 1870, Camp Stambaugh was established to provide a more permanent military presence in the region. (Courtesy United States Geological Survey.)

Lt. Col. Henry A. Morrow. Serving as post commander at Fort Bridger from 1867 to 1869, Colonel Morrow oversaw the deployment of soldiers to the South Pass gold fields. He later superintended detachments sent to guard railroad surveyors and construction crews for the new Union Pacific Railroad. (Courtesy Robert Kotchian.)

Officers at Fort Bridger. Lt. Col. (brevet Brig. Gen.) Charles C. Gilbert, standing fourth from right, served as post commander at Fort Bridger in 1869–1870. Capt. Henry R. Mizner at far left shows off his bicycle. The photograph was taken by Charles R. Savage in July 1869. (Courtesy National Archives.)

A View of Officers' Row. Families gather outside the officers' quarters at Fort Bridger in this view by photographer Charles R. Savage. Several daughters of Judge Carter are visible at left. (Courtesy Wyoming State Archives.)

Officers at Fort Bridger. First Lt. Henry H. Link, 36th Infantry, standing third from right, wears a sash across his shoulder that signifies his assignment as Officer of the Day, supervising the guard over a 24-hour period. (Courtesy National Archives.)

Senior NCOs of the 36th Infantry. In 1866, the Army was reorganized, with two of the battalions of the 18th Infantry being redesignated as the 27th and the 36th Infantry. The regiment's new sergeant major and two other senior noncommissioned officers sat for their portrait in Salt Lake City about 1867. (Courtesy Fort Laramie National Historic Site, National Park Service.)

Carter's Sawmill. Among William Carter's other business ventures was cutting logs and rough lumber for use by the Army. Photographer C.R. Savage was visiting Carter's sawmill in July 1869 when a soldier accidently dumped his chemicals "thus terminating my photographic efforts in this region," Savage noted in his diary. (Courtesy Brigham Young University.)

Dr. Joseph K. Corson. Stationed at Fort Bridger from September 1870 to November 1872, the young Army doctor later married one of the daughters of Judge Carter. After retiring from the Army, Corson was awarded the Medal of Honor for his heroic action during the Civil War evacuating a wounded soldier during an artillery bombardment. (Courtesy Wyoming State Archives.)

Fort Bridger, c. 1871. Artist Anton Schonborn created this detailed watercolor view of Fort Bridger, perhaps while he was a member of the Hayden survey that disbanded at Fort Bridger in

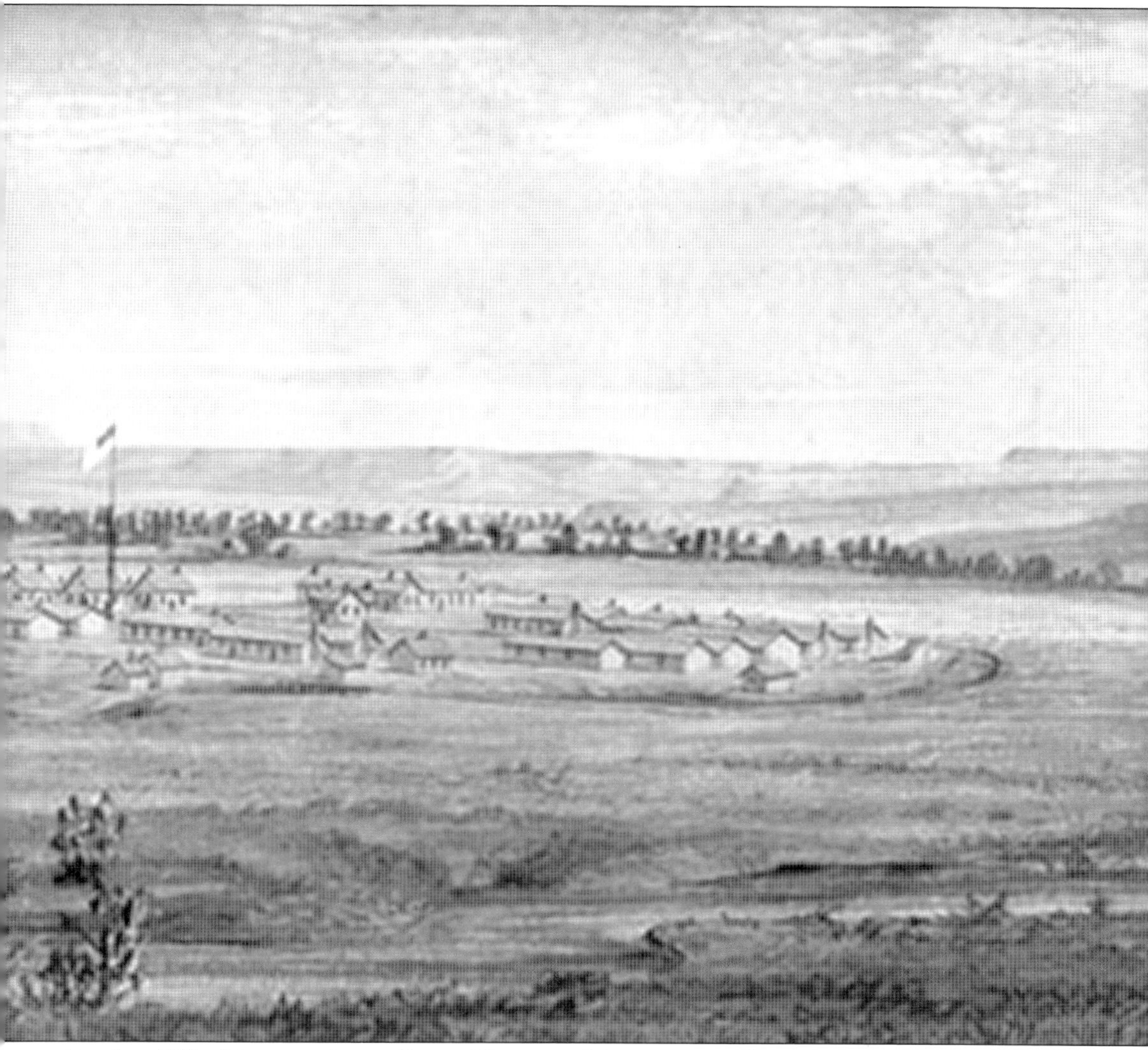

October 1871. (Courtesy Amon Carter Museum of American Art.)

Sutler Store and Warehouse. By the 1870s when this image was taken, Judge Carter's complex on the edge of Fort Bridger had expanded. The false-front building at left was probably built as a saloon and billiard parlor within the adjacent town of Merrill. Later, it served as the Enlisted Mens' Club. (Courtesy Wyoming State Archives.)

Col. Albert G. Brackett. "This is a delightful summer resort, cool and pleasant," wrote Colonel Brackett, post commander at Fort Bridger from October 1872 to May 1873. An avid outdoorsman, Bracket noted "the clear streams abounding in mountain trout, and game being plentiful up near the mountains." (Courtesy National Archives.)

COL. FRANKLIN F. FLINT. From 1873 to 1878, Fort Bridger served as regimental headquarters for the 4th Infantry, under the command of Colonel Flint. As a captain in the 6th Infantry, Flint had first traveled to Fort Bridger in 1857 as escort for the Army survey party through Bridger's Pass and returned the following year as a part of reinforcements for the Utah War. (Courtesy National Archives.)

4TH INFANTRY BAND. As regimental headquarters, Fort Bridger also received the regiment's 20-member band who provided music for various formal ceremonies as well as dances. The bandmaster can be seen standing at left. The photographer of this picture is unknown, but it was taken around 1872. (Courtesy Wyoming State Archives.)

Collecting Fossils. Professor Marsh's expedition is busy digging fossils near Fort Bridger in 1871. Charles W. Savage took the photograph. (Courtesy Brigham Young University.)

Four

The Fossil Bone Wars

While the scientific study of fossils, or paleontology, had largely developed in Europe, the unexplored rock outcrops of the American West offered tremendous potential for new finds that might help decipher the history of life. Fur trappers and later military officers at Fort Bridger soon discovered fossil bones eroding from the nearby badlands. But not until James Van Allan Carter sent a package of specimens to the noted scientist Dr. Joseph Leidy in 1868 did their true importance become widely known. Here were fossil mammals from the Eocene, dating back nearly 50 million years, a period of time not otherwise known from North America. An intense rivalry soon developed as scientists hurried to Fort Bridger in a race to discover and name the new species of ancient mammals.

In 1869, Ferdinand Hayden visited the badlands near Fort Bridger, recovering a number of new specimens that he sent to his colleague Dr. Leidy for description and publication. These reports soon caught the attention of Dr. O.C. Marsh from Yale University, who decided to organize an expedition of his own the following year. With an escort from Fort Bridger, Marsh and his 12 students searched the badlands further, shipping back a number of new discoveries. Both Hayden and Leidy were dismayed that Professor Marsh had now intruded into what they viewed as their exclusive scientific territory.

Hayden organized another expedition to Fort Bridger in 1871, as did Marsh. Eleven boxes of fossils were shipped back to Yale University, including the bones of a new ancient horse, and Marsh even hired several local residents to continue prospecting after his departure. To speed up the publication of his fossil finds, Hayden allowed another ambitious young paleontologist named Edward D. Cope to join his team. But Cope was soon operating on his own, often competing with Leidy for fossils. The rivalry intensified in 1873 as Marsh again returned to Fort Bridger. Soon, however, the intense competitiveness moved on to other fossil localities. Deeply frustrated, Dr. Leidy left paleontology altogether while the bitter rivalry between Marsh and Cope continued, soon carrying over into their search for new dinosaur bones.

The study of fossils from the Fort Bridger area continued after this initial rush. Princeton University collected here in 1877 and the American Museum of Natural History organized several expeditions between 1903 and 1906. Numerous universities continue to visit the region even today. To date, more than 67 different genera of mammals have been identified as well as many species of turtles, lizards, crocodiles, and fish.

Joseph Leidy. Professor of anatomy at the University of Pennsylvania in Philadelphia, Dr. Leidy was one of the foremost authorities on vertebrate fossils, publishing several major early works on ancient reptiles and mammals discovered throughout the American West. (Courtesy National Archives.)

***Omomys carteri*.** In 1868, J. Van Allan Carter sent a package of small bones from the Fort Bridger area to Dr. Leidy for study, including what proved to be a small jaw of the first fossil primate from North America. Leidy's publication of the species, named after Carter, helped bring the Fort Bridger badlands to the attention of the scientific community. (Courtesy University of Kansas.)

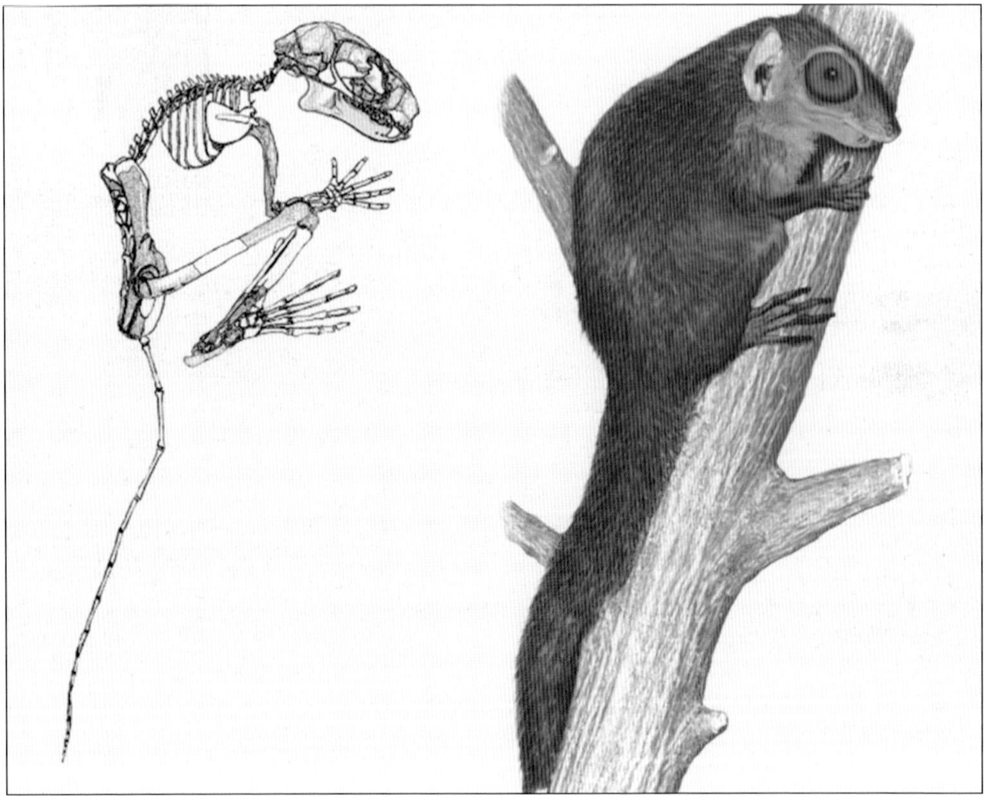

Church Buttes. Carter was soon joined on his fossil expeditions by the newly arrived Army surgeon, Dr. Joseph Corson. "We found many most interesting remains," Corson later recalled, "and the fame of Leidy's discoveries brought on us a succession of enthusiastic scientists." (Courtesy Wyoming State Archives.)

Ferdinand Hayden. After the Civil War, Ferdinand Hayden continued his pioneering studies of the geology of the West, making his first visit to the Fort Bridger area in 1869. "There are indications that when this group is thoroughly explored it will prove second only to the Bad Lands of Dakota in the richness and extent of the vertebrate remains," he wrote. (Courtesy United States Geological Survey.)

Church Buttes. One of the key localities from which the Hayden Expedition collected fossil turtles and mammals was at Church Buttes, located about 15 miles east of Fort Bridger. Fossils collected on this expedition were shipped to Dr. Leidy for description and publication. (Courtesy United States Geological Survey.)

MEMBERS OF THE HAYDEN SURVEY, 1870. Ferdinand Hayden returned in 1870 with a larger expedition, traveling overland through South Pass to Fort Bridger and then back to Cheyenne. This image shows his crew encamped near Red Buttes, about 300 miles northeast of Fort Bridger. (Courtesy United States Geological Survey.)

CHURCH BUTTES. For this second view, photographer William H. Jackson turned his camera to the right to capture the remainder of this distinctive rock outcrop. Church Buttes was a commonly mentioned landmark along the Overland Trail and was frequently photographed by traveling artists. (Courtesy United States Geological Survey.)

William Henry Jackson. Having just completed a special photographic commission for the Union Pacific Railroad, Jackson was invited to join Hayden on his 1870 adventure, but without pay. His success on this trip earned him a permanent position on the survey and boosted his growing reputation as one of the country's foremost landscape artists. (Courtesy United States Geological Survey.)

Camp near Church Buttes. Hauling their supplies by wagon and mule, Hayden's survey teams spent months living in tents, pressing plant samples, preparing taxidermy skins, and labeling mineral and fossil specimens to be shipped back East. (Courtesy United States Geological Survey.)

Badlands. Jackson's view into the Bridger Basin badlands shows the complex layering of siltstones, sandstones, limestone, and ash-fall tuff beds. While Hayden's crew only noted approximate localities for their fossils, future paleontologists developed detailed stratigraphic profiles of these rocks upon which to plot their fossil discoveries. (Courtesy United States Geological Survey.)

Badlands View. The sedimentary rocks that outcrop near Fort Bridger were laid down by ancient streams and lakes between 45.5 and 49 million years ago, a period of time geologists refer to as the Eocene. Ash layers help to date the rocks with increasing precision. This photograph was taken by William Henry Jackson in 1870. (Courtesy United States Geological Survey.)

Fossil Turtles. Among the most common and easily recognizable fossils from the Bridger Formation were the fossilized shells of land tortoises. This remarkable slab containing 15 turtles was discovered in the Bridger area by a Smithsonian field crew in 1941. (Courtesy Smithsonian Institution.)

John Wesley Powell. A professor of geology at Illinois Wesleyan University, Powell organized two student field trips to Colorado Territory in 1867 and 1868. He obtained supplies at Fort Bridger in the spring of 1869 before organizing his famous expedition down the Green River and Colorado River through the Grand Canyon. (Courtesy National Archives.)

OTHNIEL C. MARSH. Professor of vertebrate paleontology at Yale University, Marsh brought three student expeditions to the Fort Bridger area between 1870 and 1873, recovering a number of new vertebrate fossils. (Courtesy Library of Congress.)

Fossil Collecting, 1871. In this detail of a photograph by Salt Lake City photographer Charles R. Savage, members of Marsh's field crew can be seen digging up fossils to send back to Yale University. (Courtesy Brigham Young University.)

Orohippus. During his 1871 expedition, Marsh and his students discovered two species of a new early horse that he named *Orohippus*. This reconstruction of what the small mammal looked like was painted by the famed paleontological illustrator Charles R. Knight in 1896. (Courtesy Library of Congress.)

YALE EXPEDITION, 1873. Marsh's final trip to the Fort Bridger area came in 1873 when he again collected and shipped a number of crates of fossils back to Yale University. Discoveries of new fossils in other areas of the West soon drew his attention away from southwestern Wyoming. (Courtesy Wyoming State Archives.)

CLARENCE KING. As superintendent of the United States Geological Survey of the 40th Parallel, King oversaw the geological mapping along the Green River in 1871–1872. He also fitted out an expedition at Fort Bridger to examine a famous diamond claim in Colorado that he determined to have been an elaborate fraud. (Courtesy United States Geological Survey.)

Edward D. Cope. Though sometimes struggling with his health, Cope convinced Dr. Hayden to allow him to join his 1872 expedition to the Fort Bridger area but the two were soon having difficulties. By hiring two of Marsh's fossil collectors, Cope also caused hard feelings with Professor Marsh. (Courtesy National Archives.)

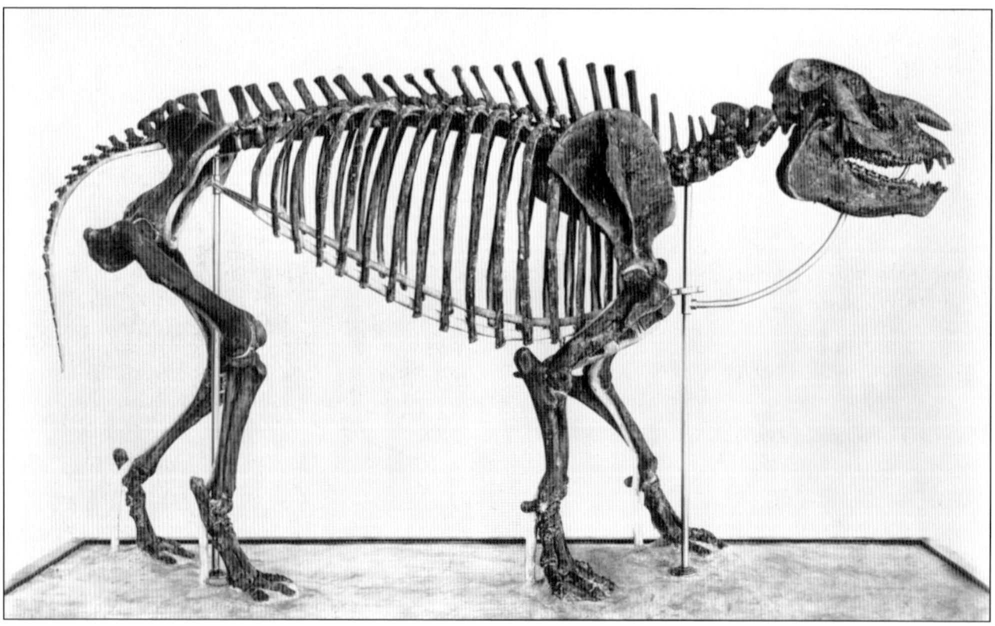

Paleosyops. One of the more common large mammals found in the Bridger beds was named *Paleosyops* by Dr. Leidy. Both Marsh and Cope later found additional specimens, including partial skulls that intensified the debate about this animal. Modern paleontologists refer this genus to an extinct group of herbivorous mammals known as brontotheres. (Courtesy American Museum of Natural History.)

Fort Bridger Croquet Party. After years of studying fossils sent to him, Dr. Leidy made his first trip west, traveling to Fort Bridger to explore the rocks for himself. He is seated seventh from the right. Shortly after his last visit to Fort Bridger, Leidy left the rancorous competition of vertebrate paleontology for other studies. (Courtesy National Archives.)

Henry Fairfield Osborn. First visiting the Fort Bridger area to collect fossils in 1877, Osborn returned several times throughout his professional career. He was among the first to have fossils collected with notes for each specimen detailing their precise stratigraphic location, allowing for finer resolution of biological change over time. (Courtesy American Museum of Natural History.)

POST QUARTERMASTER SERGEANT HORACE E. MYRICK. Arriving at Fort Bridger in 1885, Sergeant Myrick and his family served at the post until it closed in 1890. His son Horace Jr. later married a local rancher's daughter and raised his family near Fort Bridger. (Courtesy Fort Douglas Museum.)

Five

The Army's Final Years at Fort Bridger

In the spring of 1878, the military garrison at Fort Bridger was ordered to be abandoned. The two companies of the 4th Infantry, which comprised the troops at the post, vacated the fort in May. A detachment of quartermaster personnel remained at Bridger until June 11.

The Ute uprising, resulting in the death of Maj. Thomas T. Thornburgh and others in 1879, prompted the military to increase its presence in the region of the Uintah Reservation where the warring Utes had been relocated. A new military post, Fort Thornburgh, was to be built near the reservation and military planners determined Fort Bridger to be the best-situated post to provide supplies to Thornburgh. As a result, soldiers were once again sent to Fort Bridger. In June 1880, Capt. William H. Bisbee and Company H, 4th Infantry left Fort Fred Steele and traveled to their new duty station at Fort Bridger.

During the next 10 years, the soldiers at the post were kept busy with a variety of tasks. First, the troops constructed a wagon road to Fort Thornburgh, Utah Territory. Soldiers also provided the labor needed to replace wooden telegraph poles between the fort and Carter Station with iron poles. New barracks and quarters were also constructed on the post, in addition to the 1889 installation of a water system.

The soldiers also played a role in enforcing laws and maintaining order. The most notable example of this service was displayed in September 1885 when troops from Fort Bridger and elsewhere were called upon to restore order and protect property in the city of Rock Springs, Wyoming Territory, during the violent Chinese Riot. The result of this unfortunate incident was the death of 28 Chinese and the burning of the city's Chinatown. The city of Evanston, having the potential for a similar confrontation, also received protection from Fort Bridger's troops.

In 1890, the federal government made the decision to abandon a number of western military posts, Fort Bridger being one of them. On November 6 of that year, the final detachment of soldiers left the post, never to return again. The final chapter of Fort Bridger's military history had been written.

Enlisted Men's Barracks. This 1870s view looks south toward the set of six enlisted men's barracks on the south side of the fort's parade ground. The middle bridge on Groshon Fork appears near the center. Note the recently planted trees. (Courtesy Wyoming State Archives.)

View From the Middle Bridge. The set of six barracks located on the north side of the parade ground can be seen on the right. The commissary and quartermaster buildings appear opposite the bridge on the west boundary of the parade ground. This photograph is believed to date from the 1870s. (Courtesy Wyoming State Archives.)

Carter Home. This image captures the upgrades made to the front of the home of Fort Bridger's post sutler. The house now sports a front porch and a bay window. William A. Carter is pictured leaning against the fence at right. Carter died of pleurisy at his home in Fort Bridger on November 7, 1881. (Courtesy Wyoming State Archives.)

Capt. William H. Bisbee. Enlisting in the Army in 1861, Bisbee rose through the ranks to retire in 1902 as a brigadier general. Bisbee first served at Bridger in the mid-1870s. When the Army reoccupied the fort in 1880, it was Bisbee who commanded the post from that year until November 1882. Bisbee lived to be 102 years old, passing away in 1942. (Courtesy Wyoming State Archives.)

BAND QUARTERS. The band quarters can be seen behind the bridge. The building was originally constructed in the mid-1870s to house the 4th Infantry band. The structure was later utilized for other purposes. Close examination of the background near the center of the image reveals the post's bandstand under construction in 1884. (Courtesy National Archives.)

MIDDLE FOOTBRIDGE AT FORT BRIDGER. During the early years of the fort, two footbridges spanned what would become known as Groshon Fork. Later, a third bridge was constructed upstream, or to the south of the middle bridge. A street lamp can be seen at the left of this 1880s image. (Courtesy National Archives.)

Road in Front of Officers' Row. This 1880s view looks south along the front of officers' row. The picket fence and boardwalk appearing in the foreground ran the length of the row of quarters. Landscaping efforts are also quite apparent in this photograph. Close examination reveals a street lamp to the right of the boardwalk. (Courtesy National Archives.)

Officers in Front of Bandstand. A bandstand, built in 1884, was located in front of officers' row near the middle footbridge. Among the group of officers in this group photograph, believed to have been taken at Fort Bridger, is Lt. Col. A.G. Brackett, 2nd Cavalry, who served as commanding officer in 1872 and 1873. (Courtesy Wyoming State Archives.)

Commanding Officer's Quarters. Completed in 1884, these quarters not only housed the commanding officer and his family, but visiting dignitaries as well. Perhaps most notable among these was Gen. George Crook. The general, an avid outdoorsman, enjoyed his visits to the Fort Bridger area. This photograph was taken when Lt. Col. Thomas M. Anderson commanded the post. (Courtesy Wyoming State Archives.)

Rock Springs Chinese Riot. Col. Alexander McDowell McCook, pictured at far right, led a contingent of soldiers to Rock Springs, Wyoming Territory, in early September 1885 to restore order and protect property following the Chinese Riot, which resulted in the death of 28 Chinese. The military presence included soldiers from Fort Bridger. At the time of the riot, soldiers from the region were engaged in a camp of instruction in Weber Canyon, Utah Territory. (Courtesy Union Pacific Railroad Museum.)

FORT BRIDGER SOLDIERS. This is a Baker and Johnston photograph of enlisted men from Company B, 9th Infantry dating from the 1880s. The men sport both military and civilian headwear. Marksmanship had become a priority to the Army and a number of marksman's buttons appear on the soldiers' collars. The two soldiers at left also wear sharpshooter's pins. (Courtesy Wyoming State Archives.)

FORT BRIDGER ENLISTED MEN. This studio portrait of six privates from Company B 9th Infantry was also taken by Evanston photographers Baker and Johnston in the 1880s. Once again, marksman's buttons are prevalent. (Courtesy Wyoming State Archives.)

Fort Bridger, 1886. This photograph of Fort Bridger looking from south to north offers a rare view of the entire fort on the west side of Groshon Fork. Of particular interest are the rear portions of the enlisted men's barracks, something seldom captured on film. (Courtesy National Archives.)

A Different view of Fort Bridger, 1886. Taken at the same time as the previous image, the photographer has turned his camera to the right, capturing the commanding officer's quarters at the far right. A portion of the post's L-shaped hospital can be seen at the extreme right. (Courtesy National Archives.)

Cpl. James McLean. Foreign-born and of Irish descent, something quite common in the frontier Army, McLean rose to the rank of first sergeant in Company D, 21st Infantry before being discharged in 1888 at Fort Bridger. In this photograph dating from around 1886, McLean's collar sports a pair of marksman's buttons. (Courtesy Wyoming State Archives.)

On Officers' Row. Civilians pose with officers from the 8th Infantry and possibly the 4th Infantry in front of officers' quarters along officers' row on the east side of the post in 1886. (Courtesy National Archives.)

Buglers at Fort Bridger. A soldier's daily life was dictated by the calls of the bugler. These men's instruments notified the rank and file when it was time to awake, when it was mealtime, and when to retire at night. The buglers also announced various duties throughout the day, among other informative calls. This image dates to around 1888. (Courtesy Wyoming State Archives.)

Officers at Bridge. A group of officers at Fort Bridger pose for this photograph taken in the 1880s. Groshon Fork provided a physical barrier between the enlisted ranks and the officer corps, reinforcing the military's caste-like culture. (Courtesy Wyoming State Archives.)

FORT BRIDGER, 1889. This panoramic painting of Fort Bridger by Merritt D. Houghton shows the fort as it appeared shortly before its abandonment. The Oregon-California-Mormon Trail can be seen in the foreground. Officers' Row and the Carter complex are on the left. The parade

ground, surrounded by enlisted men's barracks, can be seen near the right in the center. (Courtesy Wyoming State Archives.)

Pump House and Water Tank. This undated photograph shows the pump house and water tank associated with the water system that was installed throughout Fort Bridger in 1889, a year before it was vacated. These structures were located on the southern edge of the fort. (Courtesy Wyoming State Archives.)

Pump House Interior. This interior view of the pump house was taken in 1916 and shows part of the mechanism that propelled the fort's water system when it still functioned as an active military post. (Wyoming State Archives.)

Group of Officers and Civilians. Officers from the 17th and 21st Infantry appear in front of W.A. Carter's store at Fort Bridger. This image was taken in 1889, as a fire hydrant can be seen at far left. Two civilians, Maurice Groshon at extreme right and W.A. Carter Jr., wearing a derby hat, would play prominent roles in the development of the town of Fort Bridger. (Courtesy Wyoming State Archives.)

Blacks Fork Bridge. A bridge across the Blacks Fork helped travelers along the Fort Bridger-to-Carter road. Fort Bridger is visible in the background. A telephone line connecting the fort with Carter was installed in the 1880s, being the first telephone utilized by the military in the territory and one of the earliest used in the territory in general. Charles R. Savage took the photograph. (Courtesy Brigham Young University.)

Meals 35¢. An unidentified group poses for the camera in front of a Fort Bridger eating house during the earliest days of the town's existence. Dining establishments would remain a fixture in the town's landscape. (Courtesy Wyoming State Archives.)

Six

The Town of Fort Bridger Emerges

The Army's abandonment of Fort Bridger signaled significant changes for Bridger Valley. The military reservation, consisting of 16 square miles, passed into the hands of the Department of the Interior. At the time of the transfer, the fort contained 51 buildings valued at $27,735. The garrison and the land surrounding the post now became available for settlement. In 1892, the buildings from the fort were sold to the public. Many of the buildings were moved from the fort to serve the needs of the residents in the area, while other structures remained on the site.

The town of Fort Bridger as it is known today developed slowly, as it took time to claim federal land and then prove up on those claims. Judge Carter's widow, Mary E. Carter, remained at the family home at Fort Bridger, while her son-in-law Maurice Groshon operated the family store.

In the late 1800s, the first surveyed town site in the vicinity of the former garrison was the community of Bridger, located a mile east of the former post. The small town included two stores, two blacksmith shops, a school, a hotel and restaurant, a saloon and poolroom, and a building that served as a dance hall and community church.

Bridger was short-lived, however, due to the efforts of William A. Carter Jr., who owned property next to the old fort. He divided the land into lots and then sold them. Carter also opened a store in the former fort's commissary. Most of the population of Bridger, as well as others from the surrounding area, moved to the new community where they established homes and businesses. The present town of Fort Bridger thus came into existence. With the establishment of the Lincoln Highway through the town, the future of the community was assured.

The town of Carter located on the route of the Union Pacific Railroad continued to serve the area as a major shipping center. Other settlements, most notably Mountain View and Lyman, emerged after the Army's departure. Canal building and irrigation efforts greatly enhanced the agricultural possibilities of the vicinity and secured the growth of ranches and communities throughout Bridger Valley.

POST SUNDIAL. Following the Army's departure from the fort, much of the government's property was sold at auction to the general public. The post sundial, for instance, was acquired for the use of the Carter family. The dial was moved from its original location to an area closer to the Carter home. (Courtesy Butch and Nancy Kahus.)

OFFICERS AND CIVILIANS. Three unidentified officers pose for a studio portrait with two civilians. The gentleman at left is believed to be Frank Hinkey. The man at right is Judge William Alexander Carter's son W.A. Carter Jr. (Courtesy Wyoming State Archives.)

MARY E. CARTER. In 1848, Mary wed William Alexander Carter. The couple made Fort Bridger their home and raised six children there. After her husband's death in 1881, she continued the family business at the fort. When the post was abandoned in 1890, Mrs. Carter remained and finally received title to her property there in 1896. She passed away in 1904. (Courtesy Wyoming State Archives.)

THE CASTO HOME. This beautiful house, once located at the fort, served the William Casto family as their home. The building, former officers' quarters, is but one example of a military structure being procured by the local populace for private use after the fort's abandonment. Casto is pictured at far left holding a child's hand and standing next to former Fort Bridger soldier John "Mac" McLaughlin. (Courtesy Butch and Nancy Kahus.)

THE LANE HOME. W.T. Lane served as a blacksmith in the first town in the vicinity of the former post, known simply as Bridger. He moved his business to Fort Bridger once the area at the former military post could be settled. He also built a dance hall there. (Courtesy Wyoming State Archives.)

THE GOODRICK-ARTHUR HOME. This house is yet another example of a former Fort Bridger officers' quarters being utilized as a home after the Army's departure. This photograph shows the building as it appeared around 1930. The house may be seen today on the grounds of the Fort Bridger State Historic Site. (Courtesy Wyoming State Archives.)

The Groshon Home. Maurice Groshon played an instrumental role in the development of the town of Fort Bridger and the subsequent historic site as well. Married to one of Judge William Alexander Carter's daughters, Groshon continued to operate the family's store in the years after Carter's death. (Courtesy Wyoming State Archives.)

Funeral Procession to Fort Bridger Cemetery. The cemetery is located just left of the photographer's position. The fort's first cemetery was situated northeast of the post but was moved in the late 1860s to its current location, approximately one mile southeast of the fort. In May 1891, a total of 23 soldiers' graves were moved from the site to Fort McPherson Military Cemetery in Nebraska. (Courtesy Butch and Nancy Kahus.)

The William Alexander Carter Jr. Home. This modest home belonged to Judge Carter's eldest son. In addition to caring for the family's varied business affairs after his father's death, Carter laid out the town of Fort Bridger in the early 1900s and was later prominent in the development of the former fort becoming a historical landmark. This photograph dates from the 1920s. (Courtesy Wyoming State Archives.)

Fort Bridger Dance Hall. The large building pictured at right served the community as a dance hall. The structure was located on the east side of town. The road passing in front of the dance hall leads to the cemetery. The unidentified building at left is situated approximately where the post office currently stands. This image was taken in 1920. (Courtesy Wyoming State Archives.)

Fort Bridger Guardhouse. This 1920s photograph shows modifications made to the former guardhouse in order to meet the needs of its civilian owner. The building would also see use as the local American Legion hall into the 1960s. The guardhouse was eventually restored to reflect its intended use. (Courtesy Wyoming State Archives.)

The 1888 Barracks. Modifications are once again evident in this 1926 image of the former stone enlisted men's barracks. At one time after the Army's departure the building was used as a dairy barn. The old post commissary is pictured at right. The barracks now serves as the fort's museum. (Courtesy Wyoming State Archives.)

Fort Bridger Ruins. This image of the rear portion of the 1868 guardhouse, taken in the 1920s, reveals early efforts to preserve the structure as evidenced by the support beams propped against the wall. Also pictured are the remnants of the "Mormon Wall," a section of the Mormon stockade utilized by the Army as a portion of the commissary's north wall. (Courtesy Sweetwater County Historical Museum.)

Rear Portions of Barracks, Commissary, and Guardhouse. A more distant view of the same area as pictured in the previous photograph, also taken in the 1920s. The back of the commissary building appears at left. That section of the building no longer exists. Pictured at right is a portion of the 1888 barracks, the current museum building. (Courtesy Sweetwater County Historical Museum.)

1888 Barracks. The 1888 stone barracks are pictured here as seen from the back of the building in the 1920s. The dormer placed in the roof is an alteration to the structure made by its civilian owner after the post's abandonment. (Sweetwater County Historical Museum.)

Carter Home, 1920s. The Carter home was known far and wide for its amenities and for the hospitality of its owners. Sadly, the house was lost to a fire in 1931. This photograph shows the back of the home. The chimney is a remnant from a section of the post sutler's store that had been previously destroyed. (Courtesy Sweetwater County Historical Museum.)

Carter Garden. Pictured from left to right are Margaret Roe, Dr. T.H. Roe, William A. Carter Jr., and Ira Rochford. All were prominent members of the early community of Fort Bridger but none more so than Carter. No other individual had a greater impact on the existence of the town. (Courtesy Wyoming State Museum.)

Fort Bridger Store. This unidentified store in 1920s Fort Bridger exemplifies the popular false-front architecture so prevalent in the 19th-century American West. (Courtesy Wyoming State Archives.)

Orange and Black Cabins. Cliff Robinson and Oscar Dahlquist stand at the office of the Orange and Black Cabins, built around 1920. With the establishment of the Lincoln Highway in the early 1900s, tourism became an important part of the Fort Bridger economy. The Rochford family operated the motel for a number of years. (Courtesy Wyoming State Archives.)

Cecil Robinson Garage. The advent of the automobile witnessed the end of the blacksmith and the rise of the automobile garage. The Robinson Garage met the needs of not only the local populace, but also travelers and tourists passing through along the Lincoln Highway. (Courtesy Wyoming State Archives.)

The Relic. This store, owned by William Casto, served the needs of the local community and, as the signage indicates, also catered to the needs of tourists. This photograph was taken around 1920. Note the early gasoline pump at right. (Courtesy Butch and Nancy Kahus.)

Rochford Hotel at Fort Bridger. The commanding officer's quarters was moved a short distance to the east of its original location and converted into a hotel in the town of Fort Bridger. The structure was dismantled after its days as a hotel and was then reconstructed on its original site and opened to the public in the 1980s. This photograph was taken by Emil Kopac on October 29, 1931. (Courtesy Denver Public Library.)

The 1880 Commissary and Quartermaster Store House. The former commissary and quartermaster buildings were utilized by William Alexander Carter Jr. for his Fort Bridger store operation. Later, W.H. Harvey owned the buildings, which appeared much as they did when the Army owned them. (Courtesy Wyoming State Archives.)

FORT BRIDGER CAFE. Later in the 20th century, the 1880 commissary operated as a café under the stewardship of John Dahlquist, feeding locals as well as tourists traveling on US Highway 30. The Dahlquist homestead cabin had been moved to the site and can be seen at left. (Courtesy Wyoming State Archives.)

FORT MOTEL. This 1962 image of the former commissary and quartermaster buildings shows further development of the structures. The commissary continued to function as a café and the larger storehouse behind it became a motel. Today, these buildings belong to the state of Wyoming and serve as the historic site's administrative and curatorial buildings. (Courtesy Wyoming State Archives.)

Fort Bridger Historical Marker. Due in large part to well-known Wyoming historian Grace Raymond Hebard and the Wyoming Oregon Trail Commission, this monument was erected near the present entrance to the fort in 1914. Hebard recommended that monuments be placed at notable Oregon Trail landmarks across the state of Wyoming. The original plaque on the monument has since been replaced. The Fort Bridger Hotel, also known as the Rochford Hotel, appears in the background. (Courtesy Sweetwater County Historical Museum.)

Seven

The Fort Becomes a Historic Landmark

By the late 1920s, interest in preserving the historic landmarks in the state of Wyoming led to the creation of the Historic Landmark Commission of Wyoming. More specifically, the movement was based on a desire to save Fort Laramie for the benefit of future generations. From this initial interest in preserving one fort, a number of historic sites throughout the state—including Fort Bridger—were recognized.

Through the commission's efforts, in 1928, Fort Bridger became the third property in the state to be set aside for preservation. Fort Reno and Connor Battlefield, both located in northern Wyoming, had been secured the previous year. In late June 1928, Maurice Groshon, Judge Carter's son-in-law, conveyed more than 30 acres of the post to Warren Richardson of Cheyenne and Robert Ellison of Casper. These men represented the Historic Landmark Commission. The property was placed in escrow and the commission received the deed to the land on April 3, 1929. About two months later, Mr. and Mrs. William A. Carter Jr. donated two lots located at the fort's present entrance to the commission. Lastly, in 1930, the land encompassing officers' row and the bandstand area was purchased from William C. Casto.

In June 1933, the Fort Bridger Museum, located in the former post sutler's store, was formally dedicated, and the fort itself was recognized as a historic landmark. A number of dignitaries attended the event, most notable among them the famous Western artist and photographer William Henry Jackson. Attendance estimates for the event ranged from 5,000 to 12,000 people, an assemblage considered to be the largest group ever to gather for any purpose in Uinta County's history up to that time.

August 1951 witnessed another large gathering at the fort, this time to dedicate the new museum at the post. The historic site's collections were moved and exhibited in the stone barrack building, which continues to serve as Fort Bridger's museum today.

Another milestone in the historic site's development came in 1972 when the first Fort Bridger Rendezvous was held at the site. The rendezvous has become an annual event hosted at the fort every year during the first weekend in September. Thousands of visitors flock to the small community for the mountain man gathering.

Today, the Fort Bridger State Historic Site continues to inform the visiting public about all aspects of the fort's past. During the late 1970s and early 1980s, two original buildings, the commanding officer's quarters and the Goodrick House, were returned to the site and a replica of the fort's bandstand was constructed. In addition to the museum, the buildings at the post have been refurnished with period furniture and related artifacts. Also, a reconstructed replica of Jim Bridger's trading post offers visitors an education in the history of Fort Bridger during the fur trade era.

Fort Bridger, c. 1917. This view, taken from the site's current entrance, shows the 1914 historical marker standing prominently in the foreground just a few short years after its placement. The post sutler's complex can be seen at right. The lone surviving officers' quarters appears directly behind the automobile. (Courtesy Wyoming State Archives)

Maurice Groshon. Groshon, Judge William Alexander Carter's son-in-law, conveyed 30 acres of Fort Bridger property to representatives of the Historical Landmark Commission of Wyoming. It was through the concern and generosity of Groshon and other property owners that the historic fort survived and is preserved today. (Courtesy Wyoming State Archives.)

Early Preservationists. This photograph was taken June 29, 1928, by Maurice Groshon, two days after he conveyed the 30 acres of fort property to Warren Richardson and R.S. Ellison. The two men then placed the land in escrow to the Historical Landmark Commission of Wyoming. Richardson is pictured second from left and Ellison stands at far right. (Courtesy Wyoming State Archives.)

Members of the Commission. On May 23, 1931, members of the Historical Landmark Commission of Wyoming met at Fort Bridger. Pictured from left to right are Warren Richardson, former Wyoming governor and commission chairman B.B. Brooks, and commission secretary J.S. Weppner. A portion of the original Mormon stockade appears in the background. (Courtesy Wyoming State Archives)

Dignitaries at Pony Express Marker Dedication. In the following summer of 1932, a Pony Express marker dedication took place at the fort. Pictured from left to right are former Fort Bridger soldier John McLaughlin, Richardson, Weppner, Brooks, Groshon, W.A. Carter Jr., and Mr. Greenberg. Carter and his wife, Katherine, gave the Historical Landmark Commission of Wyoming two lots of lands near the fort's current entrance. The group poses near the 1860s commissary and guardhouse. (Courtesy Wyoming State Archives.)

William Alexander Carter Jr. Carter stands in the foreground during the festivities associated with the placement of the Pony Express marker at Fort Bridger on June 5, 1932. In addition to donating land to the commission for the establishment of the historic landmark, Carter also laid out the town of Fort Bridger on land adjacent to where his father had surveyed the town of Merrill. (Courtesy Wyoming State Archives.)

Guardhouse and Dedication Crowd. One June 25, 1933, Fort Bridger was formally dedicated as a Historical Landmark of Wyoming. The new museum was also dedicated the same day, as was the American Legion Post Home. Thousands of people attended the event. The porch on the guardhouse served as the speakers' stage. (Courtesy Wyoming State Archives.)

Flag Raising at the Dedication. The festivities marking the dedication of the landmark and museum included a formal flag raising ceremony. According to one source, the flag used was the last one flown by the Army on the fort's last day as an active military post. The dedication amassed more attendance than any other event in Uinta County's history. (Courtesy Wyoming State Archives.)

Barracks and Dedication Crowd. The large crowd assembled near the guardhouse enjoys the activities associated with the event held on June 25, 1933. A large bass drum can be seen at center, indicating the presence of a band at the dedication. The barracks, which serves as the current museum, appears in the background. (Courtesy Wyoming State Archives.)

Governor Miller at the Dedication. Wyoming governor Leslie A. Miller poses with a group of dedication attendees next to the lone remaining officers' quarters on the site. Miller is at center, directly in front of the tree. (Courtesy Wyoming State Archives.)

Dignitaries at the Dedication. The program for the dedication included speeches by an impressive array of dignitaries. In this image, a group of them has assembled at the Fort Bridger Hotel, which originally functioned as the commanding officer's quarters. From left to right are J.S. Weppner, Governor Miller, former Wyoming governor B.B. Brooks, and Warren Richardson. (Courtesy Wyoming State Archives.)

Dignitary Group at Dedication. In addition to the important figures mentioned previously, two men of note appear in this image. Famed frontier artist and photographer William Henry Jackson stands at extreme left, and Church of Latter Day Saints president Heber Grant is third from left. (Courtesy Wyoming State Archives.)

William Henry Jackson Addresses Crowd. Jackson was no stranger to Fort Bridger. In 1866, he passed through the area on his way west, making sketches along the route. In 1869, he was commissioned by the Union Pacific Railroad to photograph the scenery traversed by its rails. As a member of the 1870 and 1871 Hayden Surveys, Jackson became further acquainted with the fort. (Courtesy Wyoming State Archives.)

LDS President Grant During Speech. Among the distinguished speakers at the dedication ceremonies was Church of Latter Day Saints president Heber Grant. The site had served as an important bastion for the church in the 1850s. Grant and the other speakers addressed the crowd from the front of the fort's guardhouse. (Courtesy Wyoming State Archives.)

Former Governor at Fort Bridger. Bryant B. Brooks served as Wyoming's seventh governor from 1905 to 1911. Brooks became chairman of the Wyoming Historical Landmark Commission in 1931. He resigned from the commission in 1939. The former governor's wife, Mary, also took an active role in preserving the state's history. (Courtesy Wyoming State Archives.)

FORT BRIDGER STATE MUSEUM. The first museum at Fort Bridger was located in the remaining portion of William Alexander Carter's post sutler store. The structure was originally an L-shaped building. The chimney from the store still stands in the background. The museum remained in this building until 1951. (Courtesy Wyoming State Archives.)

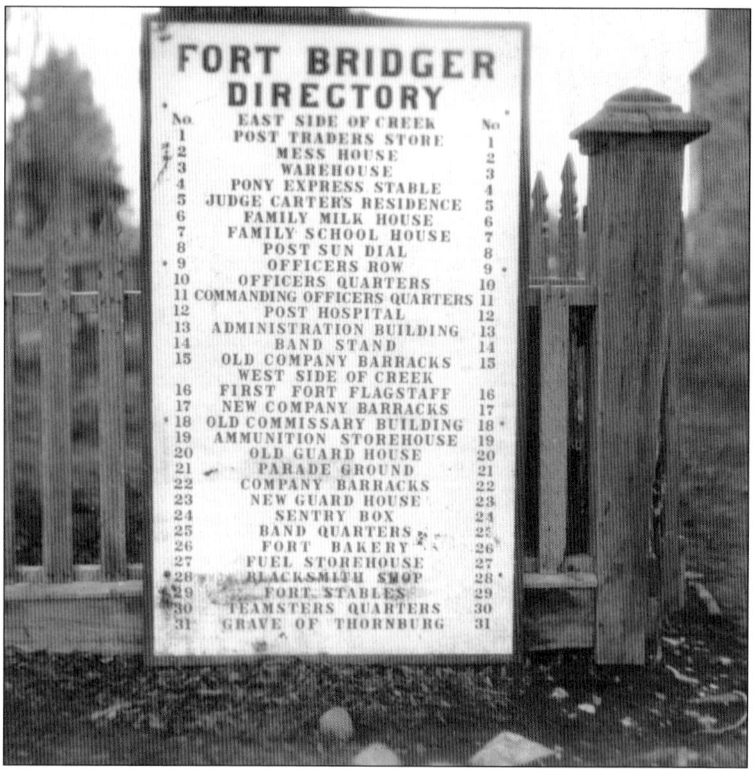

FORT BRIDGER DIRECTORY. Once located at the historic site's entrance near the museum at the Carter store, this directory listed existing landmarks as well as features that had disappeared long before. The sign represented an early effort to interpret the site to the visiting public. (Courtesy Wyoming State Archives.)

Historic Site Entrance. This view of the museum and surrounding buildings is near the present entrance to the fort. The structures appear much as they do today, with the exception of the store's chimney, which no longer stands. Note the flag pole near right center, evidently placed there due to its close proximity to the museum, as it was not a historical feature. (Courtesy Wyoming State Archives.)

Carter Family Cemetery. Originally located outside the historic site's boundary a short distance south of its current location, the cemetery was relocated in 1933 next to the commanding officer's quarters due to the Historical Landmark Commission. In addition to the Carter family, local mountain man John Robertson and Virginia Bridger Hahn, one of Jim Bridger's daughters, are buried here. (Courtesy Wyoming State Archives)

Fort Bridger Entrance. This large entry sign to the fort was placed in the mid-1960s and greeted visitors to the historic site until it was removed in the early 1980s. (Courtesy Wyoming State Archives.)

Further Reading

Alter, F. Cecil. *Jim Bridger.* Norman, OK: University of Oklahoma Press, 1962.

Bagley, Will. *So Rugged and Mountainous: Blazing the Trails to Oregon and California, 1812–1848.* Norman, OK: University of Oklahoma Press, 2010.

Bigler, David L. and Will Bagley. *The Mormon Rebellion: America's First Civil War, 1857–1858.* Norman, OK: University of Oklahoma Press, 2011.

Ellison, Robert S. *Fort Bridger: A Brief History.* Cheyenne, WY: Wyoming State Archives, Museums and Historical Department, 1981.

Gardner, Dudley. Wyoming History: "Lincoln Highway." www.wwcc.wy.edu. May 15, 2012.

Gowan, Fred R. and Eugene E. Campbell. *Fort Bridger: Island in the Wilderness.* Provo, UT: Brigham Young University Press, 1975.

Gowan, Fred R. and Eugene E. Campbell. *Fort Supply: Brigham Young's Green River Experiment.* Provo, UT: Brigham Young University Publications, 1976.

Hamblin, Kathaleen K. *Bridger Valley: A Guide to the Past.* Mountain View, WY: K.K. Hamblin, 1993.

Jording, Mike. *A Few Interested Residents: Wyoming Historical Markers & Monuments.* Helena, MT: Falcon Press Publishing Company, 1992.

Knight, Dennis H. *Mountains and Plains: The Ecology of Wyoming Landscapes.* New Haven, CT: Yale University Press, 1994.

Larson, T.A. *Wyoming: A History.* New York, NY: W.W. Norton & Co., 1977.

Lauritzen, Ruth. "Green River, WY." Interview, July 12, 2012.

Long, E.B. *The Saints and the Union: Utah Territory During the Civil War.* Urbana, IL: University of Illinois Press, 1981.

Murray, Robert A. *Military Posts of Wyoming.* Fort Collins, CO: Old Army Press, 1974.

Record Group 94. Records of the Adjutant General's Office. Post Returns, Fort Bridger. Washington, DC: National Archives.

Sandweiss, Martha A. *Print the Legend: Photography and the American West.* New Haven, CT: Yale University Press, 2002.

Shurtleff, Wallace Vincent. *Bridger Country.* Lyman, WY: Gloria Jensen, 1979.

Stone, Elizabeth Arnold. *Uinta County, Its Place in History.* Laramie, WY: Laramie Printing Company, 1924.

Thomson, Keith. *The Legacy of the Mastodon: The Golden Age of Fossils in America.* New Haven, CT: Yale University Press, 2008.

Wyoming Press. Evanston, WY: 1907.

INDEX